A.A. CLEARY

# MEN HOMEWARD

CEOLFRITH PRESS
SUNDERLAND
1977

# MEN HOMEWARD

CEOLFRITH PRESS



First Edition August 1977 Ceolfrith 41

*'Men Homeward' has been grant aided by the Arts Council of Great Britain*

The cover illustration is 'Londonderry, Ireland', c. 1833, by T.M. Baynes, engraved by W. Watkins. Reproduced by kind permission of Ulster Folk and Transport Museum.

'Men Homeward' is published in an edition of 500 copies
ISBN 0 904461 35 1 £1.50

Printed by E.F. Peterson, 12 Laygate, South Shields.
Distributed by Ceolfrith Press, Sunderland Arts Centre, 17 Grange Terrace, Stockton Road, Sunderland SR2 7DF, Tyne and Wear, England.

**CONTENTS** **page**

## ELEMENTS OF CHOICE

"–ism"'s I hate,
Because they hate. Most deprecate
All logic in the rest. And more
Deny the smallest wisdom in the ones before.
"–ism"'s, like a light sleepers ears muffled in cotton,
Turn real sound to waste, more baffled than forgotten.

"–ity"'s are really states of being, gone through:
Graces, disasters fallen on this tilted crew
Who running see some pearly patches hold
In place a sky storm takes for its pestle bowl.
"–ity"'s I like: under a quiet moon's pull tides flow;
In states of seeming stillness all things grow.

## ASYLUM

Who need it find it: refuge –
pitiable it might be thought as any fear
could be that dogged them – some little sphere
Apart, some known and guileless subterfuge
Time must collapse. To love one here
And be loved's this. Although the year
And hour it breaks will bring heart's deluge.

## MORNING

The raised voices at night? They were
Remorse shifting its position to make it tolerable,
The years blaming one another,
Evidence of life still,
A wintry assessment.

## FISHWIFE

Not the slither and gleam that made the difference
Between quiet words and the ranting bawl –
Though in the morning the haul of herself from bed was wordless,

But seeing the gleam harden, the slither go rigid (all
she had to sell), that forced and filled
Her lungs to scream the freshness of the moment.

## SUNDAY

Shall we go again then
To the 'Story of the Earth'
To see it reveal
Crust, mantle and core,
To hear the igneous roar
In the sedate afternoon,
To lie on the far shore
Of galaxies?
It is kinder than this suburb:
It has comforts
Of distance, of turbulence.

## POET TO SOCIOLOGIST

An Easter day
Like flying others
Time shot muffled down. Two barefoot daughters
Pad the sleepy kitchen, bring
Five linked and giggling toes
As mice to the cat, with fifteen
Closing up in zigzag suicide.

Your table indications, need:
Our need is to make wealth
Of that muffled loss; the wild nose
Quivers, points; the gundog runs
And lays as joyously
Near the burst gassy pouch
More softly carried birds – just days.

## BIRD AND SEA

They had seen pictured Agatha's soft breasts
Laid on a dish such maim could never carry,
The tragic tale so lost,
Nipple and rising mound so stylised,
That bellfounders, mistaking, took her for their saint,
Those empty weights took to themselves kind form,
By patronage had tongue that lifted them.

And the soul, sorting, rustling through words,
Sees images surrounding. Whether the words soul takes
Solicit truth or not, they now
Pile like Octobers; symbols remain, so central
That we fall on them repeatedly: notes strange
As the fantastic wings that take them on,
Valleys of water hung upon this curve.

## INTERNAL MANUAL VERSION OF FOETUS

Booted and masked he goes to her
Into this theatre hushed for a happening;
For this case calls for oddly new techniques:
Sight has to idle while the ear appraises
Flutter and throb. Something like eyes
Stalk on the tip of folded hand
To cradle the pulsing head
That all his sleight of mind must turn.

All the scene-shifting,
Those unpanicked parts,
Bring from that newcomer
No expected yell –
to their right stations must
senses try back –
On small uttered sympathies
Feelings trip and fall.
Centre stage a small heart lies
Rib-strapped like luggage.
Touched by its journey
Words reach out to silence.

## HOW LOVELY TO SEE YOU

Why don't you write a play –
Your own personalised tragedy? That way
The villain that you speak of could speak back
His vicious flip-side to your quiet track
That turns and raises miserably again,
This week-end too, your virtue and your pain.

I know I'm lucky – how you keep telling me –
And your ears flatten for my sympathy.
But my hand curls. I would sit through that play
On the seat's edge if what you let him say
Was written with half the loving care you took
Over your story – half the story book.

## ANTE-NATAL CLINIC

Only time's accident unites them here
In a hiatus of themselves. This routine, harshly lit,
Shows some rounding their nine-twelfths sphere,
Makes all seem vulgar fractions of it.

The golden pensive state (painters have seen) is stark
In them without a natural drape of family
And frame, but gravidness is the same marked
Earnest that they take unqualifyingly.

They've spent their credits though
For the time being, and being becomes harder;
They make bright stabs at personality, but know
Neither themselves nor the unintegrating other.

## HOT EVENING AT EUSTON (First moon-landing)

Some here are tensed so much
Their bulged brief-cases if touched
Might spurt with blood; and some are held as
Loose as their own day was:
All, in this unsexing heat,
Men still with that coolness, stream to meet
By clock's command obsessed trajectories.

And though man's pack for life's contingencies
They carry easy home, their feet alight
As gingerly as evenings infinite
Have proved was wise. They test that moondust
The way they feel instinctively they must,
By throwing out a word lightly to know
If sun was kind, making its reflection so.

## THINKING OF ELDERFLOWERS

(On the launching of a Polaris submarine, by Lady Zuckerman on November 4th, 1967, with a bottle of elderberry wine)

As days slot in and thus a life resemble
So bolts lock home. Twelve hours tie up
A wife's new winter coat. And trains assemble
A hand-picked winter crew. While ribbons loop,
Smiles, polite interest, make
Visible decorations where the questions break.

Unbroached, the complex and dichotomous story
– the splash of that red wine? – still troubles them
The hedged around and gathered faces,
For ever, quintessential, England's glory;
Some know that often in that wine a sea of bubbles
Rise to salute the flowering mega doubles
That fritter time away across waste places.

## ACCIDENT

'Shall we move her in off the road?'
Kindly they said, appalled at the blood's flow
And feeling half that the traffic must continue
And would do her further damage.
'No, she's better here' he said,
Easing her mouth, leaving
Her hurt body in that strange arc.
'Tom, Tom' she murmurs, her grey hand crooking.
He comforts her: 'He's coming,
Your husband's coming.' The streams
Are of blood, and a single one of chastened drivers.
No hurrying family come, no ambulance yet.
She holds his hand now gladly
In place of Tom's. The hand
And voice that are here have become
That man that was good to her.

## THE RIDDANCE

That week was a May junket for she seemed
A fair that was all razzle-dazzle,
Moving away. And loving her
Was such bonanza at the wheel of fortune
He'd never hit again. The dreary booth
That splices customers in pictures was the one
They never thought to enter. Her letter now
And its dead news that she'd got rid of
His unknowing child – proof the fair happened –
Sounds like dark's barkers to him. Had it been
A message of her need she sent, or had she
Brought to life his startling likeness,
It could not have left
A fairground so deserted.

## LIKE GULLS, A MENACE AT ST. IVES

They're high on light; the place's beauty grows
Quickly on these two. But in the businesslike patios
Beauty is something other: work, and what work shows:
Bought neatness and the power to organise
Good summers send.
                                        Hard living has them pale:
I wish their dream of sharing could prevail –
We need its hope. She carefully spreads
Thinly from a khaki bag his breakfast bread;
And for her street-grey eyes
That time and winter will with greys apprise,
Here at Pednolva on this blazing day,
He's spread on blue the gold impasto bay.

## THE ARMED MEN

Tenanted by the wind they have acquired
Full health. I could embrace them, knowing
Them so well, these virile ghosts attired
In white and coloured moods, elbowing,
Coming up, a twenty-foot long surge of hired
Strength stooping and lifting, going
From gleaning to scaffolding, and some fired
By obsessions of being that are always owing
Them sunlight and folly. The wind has required –
to be seen – habitation; but now stopped blowing
It witholds a dimension from this last one not dry
That is limply disturbing. I will take this one in.

## LOOK AT THE COLOURS

The woods are full of faded couples, and the trees
Blaze on. Huge alarming autumn these
Come to admire, and yearly watching we
Have joined them now, and chastened hurry through here,
Noting the same low sun that hoodwinks the trees each year.

I think that serene couples do not talk
Of that old devastation as they walk.
Agreed not to be morbid they agree
To say 'Look at the colours' for they know
The beauty's breaking, and I think they know

It wiser to assert that beauty lies
In the fall itself, not in the thing that dies.
And some say nothing and can't help but see
The lonely sweep of things. To-day for you
I wish I could forget that winter's due.

## PAINTING FOR PLEASURE

Under the headland, lost behind the rushes,
They work long hours with the best paint and brushes,
Confident we'll admire what we already do:
The elusive beauty here; they show us nothing new.

For art's joy's in the shock the sight conveys
As it slides across a picture: we see that air-pump daze
The bird, and see the girl cared and the painter cared,
And see that he, thinking we might care too, dared

To show grief inevitable: staking on a vein of love
Even in hearts not started from that love
They start in: making the room's tensions sing
Complex and clear over the heartbreak thing.

## IN THE SHELDONIAN THEATRE

Through time these surges must have been
Persistent. I do not see their exit
From my awkward seat, though the woman in the green
Hat in front of me can see into the pit,
And in her green hat must be really clear
What happens to the surges. To me
It seems repeatedly the dancers hurry,
Their worth all in their heads like acreage quietly
Anxious some warm wind has chased across the floor
And caused to bend. They each time disappear.
I hold all here though they have found a door,
That gradual clearer through the circumstance
Of my seeing just these movements of the dance:
The swathe and – keeping time – a new troupe's flurry.

## MEN HOMEWARD

As on the sunny doorstep that dog circles,
Flattening long grass cemented over,
And somewhere settles something down at last,
So here I circle too. Like linen traced
The day is tight in its frame. Threads
Dyed in their depths wait. A bloomed loaf
With the knife close to it, a jug drawn,
A woman with her fire bright, her oak board shone,
Her soup plumping. You can telephone if you like
And we could chat: it makes no difference: until
The car door slams, your shadow darkens the hall,
When keys and briefcase go, one hand shuffling
Your letters and one catching me round,
When your odd strangeness comes, I start
To stop the turning, stitch the pattern close.

And yet I've never understood the constant
Need to be alone that some lovers exhibit:
The candlelit à deux, the 'getting away', 'just us',
The tireless honeymoon. To be together – yes;
And though an image for this singular relationship
Must founder on the page, marriage for most,
Perhaps, is being in stress and near: a little
Like the calculated thermal shift of cantilever
Arms and girders: so joined – in heat or cold they
Hold their span and give a thoroughfare.

## CHARGE-HAND

'Len Evans. Greengrocer and Fruiterer'.
The '–grocer' disappears as he steps through.
Then all the yellow letters on grimed green
Shutters fold to the side. Seven fifteen.
He hangs his jacket, puts on yesterday's overall,
Stacks rubbish – yellow-green of cabbages,
Carrots gone soft, bad oranges and lettuce
Past reviving, sweeps trimmings to the floor.

He's not Len Evans but for all they care
His customers might think so. Yet,
Like the almond tree that stands all winter,
Bearing a dripping witness to its being,
His season comes, his in November. Stands
In his blaze of colour, an easy genie. Angled to
The roof his fruits are heaped, phrased
On a dark-blue paper: purple plums, pale sharp
Sicilian lemons, black grapes; the pineapples
Hold their rich pyramids. Watch, as the bus crawls by,
This cave of light. He must be cold as we are
But he turns to make another wintry dream come true;
He will go home sometime, not yet, for now
Exotic, out of season, in the gloom,
This time's his own; he lets its petals slip.

## MAIDEN CITY

1

Good-bye commits recall.
So when a loved time's left,
Though what we abandon grows
And changes its leaves lightly,
For us it is changed no more.
Pear, apple, wing and anther,
Caught colours, move till they
Become still life,
The forsaken ambers,
Stays thus arranged and chosen.
It could be just the circle that a childhood pricked
Draws now in self-love round it,
But then why should some scene or circumstance be kept,
Some be let go?
It is the needful arbitrary eye intrigues:
I do not see it as
A sparrow dipping his tail feathers in
The pool a makeshift standpipe
And builders' rubble made.

2

Now summer grows and denses;
Its camber tilts the heart, and makes
Affections halted here bolt off
Like mercury bolting newly to itself.

Bastions not sieged cannon across,
Oak bursts us with its leaf,
Bones that were withy, framing skin's coracle,
Lock to a gull-screeched peace,

Ice-cream, the Ashwell carol on a glittering morning
Empties its Jubilate, spills out of empty walls,
And light sculls darkness
On the broadening river, this Mountjoy

Breaks again the boom to Derry,
Baleful, floating, impregnable always,
Westerlies I hardly notice,
Yet from one strong claim

To what seemed abandoned ones
This season jars still particles;
The quick's enticed and (only fall correcting)
Axle-treed back.

And every year it sunders more reality:
As that remembered place now changes
I know that I changed it more, that in my mind
There is a river, is a time, made ideal,

This banishment a wish, no accident,
And that place left – illusion, but real enough
In that it's wanted so, real as those dark-cowled men,
In glass the light pours through.

## POVERTY

Stirring gruel for the cat
Who stays in her box and seems to prefer
Held up to her a dish of what we would think of
As primarily human nourishment,
I remember the tinker women who used to come to the door
And my mother moved unfailingly by the special plea:
'a taste of flake-meal for me friend' who lay
In bits of blanket just out of the town with a baby.
Such dull food it seemed to me to celebrate with,
But there was no doubt
This was the body-blow that made her heart turn
For the kitchen. The poor begging rough soul
Who in drink would tear the shawl off another
Saw her now misfortunate,
Lying-in at a time when no oats
Jingled their music in the field's corner.
And knowing that in some house surely
That dust of summer was stored cannily, kindly,
Had come asking.
Years later I knew why she wanted it:
One came again, the same heavy smell:
'a taste of flake-meal. She's lying in the lane
with a baby. It'll bring the milk in. She has
Nothing at all. For the love of God!'

## DERRY'S WALLS

The horror of revolution
Not that it destroys
Palaces, but small decencies:
The courage of, say, Lizzie Hartin's mother
Who rose in the grey of winter
To dress that shapelessness, to put the pram out,
That Lizzie might move her eye a fraction,
Sink her chin deeper as someone passed.
Some message you could almost see
Arced between eye and brain
And made a circle you would want to call a smile.
And yet, year in, year out, from the huge head
No signal came to raise a finger.
Not Lizzie but the unseen and toiling mother
Was a beacon. Passing that awkwardness
At the door so small
You couldn't think how they would make the move
Again, people would speak
And feel stricken but lifted.
This killing is the killing of such dead
And sweetest virtue:
As if its triumph was that Lizzie's head
– poor harmless Lizzie –
No longer sat there but had terribly risen
To crush that mother in Little Richmond Street.

## A FABLE

'Dear Harmony,'
He said to Miss Warmcloud,
'You are what I need.
Come and live with me.'
And she did.
And cared for him so well,
And for their family,
And tried so hard
That she became that way.
And one morning he
Was surprised at a break in routine – no breakfast –
And looking between the sheets
He saw there Censorious, one of the Sharpfrosts,
The sort of girl he would never have married
Lying back
In the luxury he had provided as a reward for
Harmony. And he said 'You are not Harmony',
But she had moved in.

Often now he looks for Harmony,
And sometimes after walking the streets
And coming home at odd hours,
He fancies he hears her singing
There, right inside the house.
But it is really Censorious,
Softened by maybe the spring light,
Or the endurance of the leaves just before they fall,
Into trying out a little song she had once known.
But when he opens the door
And she sees his disappointment –
That she is not the one he expected to find –
The song dies on her lips.

## PEOPLE FOR THE TREES

This is the year
Of Trees for the People,
Though when there has been
A definitive count of branches,
And a re-assessment
Of the optimum tree-spread per person,
There might have to be more meaningful intercourse
At grassroots level,
For I feel that ideally
There should be a tree for each person
And a person for each tree,
Realising however
That only the machinery of a Council
For the Balancing of Trees and People
(C. BOTAP)
Could ensure this.

## LONELY MEN IN LAMBETH

Now at four o' clock the good quick smell
Of little currant cakes rises. Will the archbishop
Whose work would seem (from the box-files
piled inside the window) to be often
A delving in troubled years, examining complaints,
Details of irregularities, unhappiness,
Will he eat them sitting beneath the flock wallpaper, cold,
In state, to-morrow, when he would probably rather
Enjoy them as they come: hot, brief, uncounted?
And the men who spit and shuffle past this place –
Do they,
When the waft reaches them from the basement ventilator,
Remember their mothers
Who would rise astounded
To know they command
Here, from some afternoon long ago,
Founts of emotion?

## ON TRYING TO BE OBJECTIVE

To-morrow at visiting time the ward will miss her banter
And her bluff: her gaunt and single daughter
Is ready to go home. 'You're that much brighter, Annie.'
And Annie, for Mam's sake, has been brighter now so many
Days. She knows how far the huffing bundle walks
From empty 'home', how on the six flights up she'd talk
To anyone who'd stop, to help her get a breath. If you
Could say her spirit was a church, then the view
That each person took of her would include
The trees around the church, and from where they stood
Each would see a different growth of her personality.
Yew, blown roses, ominous elm, put these before her:
Then some will see her picturesque, vulgar as rose,
Some seeing elm fault reality, suppose
Her life the flea-hunt they think poverty, and near
The yew some will be persuaded it's the terrible tears
Of tragedy have runnelled lines in her face.
But between church and trees lies an unnoticed space,
Its perfect charge to keep her from the glib viewer.

## WORD TO A CAT

Come in, poor friend,
You who will not trust again, ever really,
Trouser-legs, for the startling
Signal of fright they beam you.
Come in, for this weather
Minces our pride:
It shivers, but will come back;
You will streak up trees again;
And in spring I'll look at the empty shelves
With a pleasure not so different
From the one that stacked autumn there –
This poignant limited rhythm
You too play out but cannot know.

Come in and settle
For a while your faulty insulation near the stove.
I couldn't tell you about winter, or why,
But recall as you cannot the cool correcting of season:
Loss and wealth, wealth and loss.
It keeps me from saying:
'I don't want to know him who would permit suffering;
He isn't my kind of God.' Cat, they have minds
But small who would like a bespoke Almighty,
Well-cut, hand-sewn, beautifully finished,
The sort of God who for you would provide
A permanent steak on the wing
(though the bird might be requiring
something other in the way of reward).

Between us what a strange relationship: tiger,
Glad of my stooping.
Trust in dependence, this saucer, my trusting,
Not in those who would prefer
To dream up their little wizard and then adore him.
Stay warm in here, for perfectly
May morning's quantity
Rises undamned by what we think we'd like,
And he's not worth the name
The uncomplex handy God
We'd hold to our conditions.

## LARGE FAMILY AT EARTH'S TABLE

I can see in your face clearly
That I have asked
Too many to this meagre meal,
Have been caught red-handed
In irresponsible behaviour
At a time that is, for women,
A watershed in liberal thinking.
I feel beholden about my too-liberal invitations
Though when those that I asked got here
I explained the position and encouraged
Their appetites to be modest.

Then I hear you say of a new freezer
And of the superiority of a certain supplier
'I can buy and plan ahead and freeze
Everything at cost price, and this firm
Slaughter their own animals which is, I feel,
Really much nicer.'

I think of my messes of potage,
The bits of monastic fish I serve,
Think that even the haul of nets is not peaceful,
Think how millions of other fans
Of herbs and oil, of wine and sunlight,
Have had to be disappointed,
Turned away at the door,
Told that life was a sell-out,
Didn't they know – that for it
Tickets were fetching appalling prices.

## MORTGAGE

All I would say is:
If we were birds
There would be silence,
No singing.

Here are
Desirable nests
Constantly improved
But closed, private.

Agonies of physicality,
But sometimes no one at home
And nothing going on
In the picture window:

Out for a short hop
From unrest,
For food, or protest
At the price of it,

Or about the overcrowding in, and
Poor construction of, adjacent nests;
No love trying out a call
That sounds like love.

A pile of bricks
By the side of the road
We inhabit if we can,
Making walls with our bricks,

Keeping the music hard
In our throats, no surging
Arm in arm of spirit, no
Sacrament, no singing.

## MOMENTUM

With her hand in mine we hit the nature trail;
The runners continue to run because they must:
I can still see the white one, over the duck that has left
The water in discomfort and is not comfortable on grass;
It cannot run, this duck; it's very old maybe;
It is happy not to fly but to watch the others,
The little grebes, the swans on this beautiful lake.
The blue sprinter is at ten minutes to Doctor Sun,
But only fifteen seconds in a fast lap; then I cannot see
Him at all till easy strain signals him other
Than the walkers on the willow-pattern bridge.
Each time he enters its red ball the sun gives him a cure
Of sweat; his singlet is soaked now
On shoulder-blades and chest; another lap
His knotty spine's mapped out with wet.

They are timing themselves:
But seem by running to extend time more,
To make the abbot's fishponds oddly moving,
To let the blackthorns and the Roman wall
Group, and take out of time's stress
This sweet daughter, to hold off
Sun leaving and night coming – much
Longer than the pressed stop-watch will record.

## WIDOW MOURNING

As a cried-out dawn
Searching peaks that have ripped her
Lights without triumph on face after face
Of the vertical telltale courses
That cut and silver there
And is contained, remote again,

When after the endless rain, rooks shudder
And flap their dampness on the low meadows,
When, weakened, the sea counts her losses,
Smooths her great sheet,
When sands are sluiced and storm-patterned,
And reeds have no nesting,

Move between dark and dark
Only shapes turbulent too.

But the shadow that's haunted
This gull in a sun-shaft's
Been gathered back now to the bird.
Easy, soft, silkily, new nets put out,
And up country
The battered corn is tied in.

## WAR PHOTOGRAPHS

'Only with these moving frames, all stills,
I touch them. Though before, I know,
Hands would have risen to the outrage of it
Not nullified their power as mine do.
When she holds out to me this broken baby,
Mine just fuss, to set the aperture, to fit a lens,
Pitifully she exposes for me these perfect negatives,
And the protected formula of the emulsion helps
This film to caress for proof the scourge of skin.
I might, at another time, have been involved here,
Later written it. But this eye-witness is
My camera's, not my own. They like –
if back home I were getting it I'd like –
Some proof. And, sure, they'll put them in a case,
More bits of war, soon curios like flint or iron worked,
Those things that cannot now recall
The arc of fear they once did.
Neither will my zoom of helplessness be fixed
In these. We've come a long way from those arrowheads:
One artefact can record the kill another makes,
Inhuman, cold. Wrongs and our sense of them
Are strafed by new ones, by the sense
That certainty's another violence, end of reflection.
So we suffer bewilderment, knowing it's not pain.
I see pain round me, and unload and seal
Faces of death that aren't explained by hate,
Rather by arrogance, nose-led to conjure hell;
Its devil comes, born opportunist,
Meets our objections with a patted contract,
And gaily robes in any makeshift place,
Then strips down slow and grins.
To work out heaven somehow, what do you do
But make selections, minor calculations?'

## THE GARDEN

How they know its limits is odd
And strangely in their eyes if you meet them
Emerging from a private lane somewhere
There is no recognition: only a staring out,
The glassy-eye treatment at your familiarity.

They know this as home, pursue their interests here,
Through the wail of spring, through winter's mist and pity,
Less and less in the house as they grow older.
But when you're busy here at something,
When you weed, they come to hand and lie
At electric stretch in the valleys between the beetroot.

These are the summer nights when you are reminded
That two chairs can never make a circle, and you bring
At least one more. Then they come and dispose themselves:
Wrapped round the honeysuckle, draped from the wormy tree
That dredges high from this old plot a bounty of apples,
In the docile and languorous postures that could fool you

Into thinking they needed something from that group
That talks quietly across the evening shadows.
This morning in the dappling light they are still there,
Waiting for the rest of the circle. Somehow their need
Has so spread to the empty chairs that I cannot look.

## SPRING SONG

1

Say 'puzzle' and you'll have it right,
Or something closer to truth I think
Than that image of a common dispenser
Of what you would like at the time.
Translate the word 'puzzle' to your prayer;
Then maybe the relationship will be more true,
The identikit picture not just what you want it to be
But at least as complex as the world is.
Say 'puzzle' when you see
Three not quite young and not quite tired men
Stare damply from the train-window on this humid day,
And say it about this evening, for now
The blackbirds at the cherries feast and sing:
They do not remember the two schoolboys
Who, sparring and larking through the rain,
Were, here in Middlesex, an hour ago,
Metamorphosed by lightning.

2

'God our Mother'
Julian of Norwich

Her conviction I think
That the idea was there
Before its embodiment,
And long before
The ultimate involvement
Through that Mary.

Then strangely ask
Of that bewilderment
So human when she lost him,
Of sadness falling through her when she could
Look up at him no more
Compassion ask of that most touching love
Of her in whom the puzzling life was laid
Of flower's minuteness and of stars' huge moving,
Earth of the earth he made.

## CANDLEMAS

Mindful of four great tragedies this year
Though one knows little of what happened there
The distress being unreported, the only figures to appear
Were quiet Sensation who laid mute Grief bare
Before making exit to a newer care,

Two events in Britain, two elsewhere,
And nameless isolate ones in collapse so intense
That they in black absence only declare
Something or someone has been, has once made sense
Of light, and then murmured a grief too dense,

To-night at church the irritable priest
(for he is old) gives a candle and says
'This symbolises Christ – the wax his least
And dear humanity, the small light's infinite rays
His Godhead, there through all his suffering days,

When alone and human he began to hear
What the Father only had heard: the appalling
Sob of time, some whispers of which we know being near,
The candle the strangeness of his breaking down and falling
Upon the ground of our loss, "Father" to strangeness calling.'

## NIGHT THOUGHTS

She is frightened, the old neighbour. Since nine
She has fearfully watched the milk at the door,
The newspaper untouched by her friend.
Now with her hat on she offers the key to me.
I call 'Mrs. Jones', and she calls 'Maudie, Maudie',
But she does not come up the stair. It is so cold
I try to be quite sure before I come down again
To say 'I think she's gone. She seems
Not to have stirred at all', and put
My arm round her, so diminished, trembling.
'What shall we do with the milk?' she says.
'I won't go up. I would rather
Remember her as she was.' I say 'Take the milk',
And she does, glad that one thing is settled.
She goes back to her kitchen, for at the front
The police make a spectacle. They're a worry,
Even though they tiptoe about
And take off their crime-caps at the gate
For what was such a gentle death.

But to-night the fog creeps
And I cannot warm,
Too aware of the gaps
Between the quiet deaths and the tidy interments.
Some night I shall be afraid
To lay down my head to peace when I don't know
What poor soul will have to say 'Quite peacefully',
And carry with them my empty face
Shocked at its gentle horror.

So you who say you can face death and need no consoling,
Consider still: it is not your nerves to which strength must come
On the cold November day they find you.
And the one who uncovers your dying
To close it in again may not be so brave,
May need consolation, that this is a debt no
Bequeathing covers. One just can't know
What heart, quaking, will have to be steady,
Telling some old neighbour 'You take the milk',
What mind's eye in solitude
Our wreckage will haunt for a bit.
We can ask that the arm of God
Go round that person, unable to sleep,
Who will carry the ice of our hands
When they strew no more living,
Suddenly in the night
Dead as Caesar.

## THROUGH FITTING SKIN-COATS

Through fitting skin-coats maybe
We come back to the cloak. Not made
To a particular measure, impersonal wrapping
For any chilled one, its destiny
Is not to be put down 'deceased's effects',
But through the care of summer sun become
Again a kindly laid down pelt, the lost
Re-membered by it as they would be
At a great supper unlike any here
For not one absent. Oh, those airs
Of desperate kindliness, could they
Stow the long bitter nights?

## RIVER TOWNS

How the soft curvings
Of these rivers
Draw to themselves
Long fascinations,
Thames and all quiet ones,
Tagus and Tiber,
Each place in its green meander apart
From the next hidden place,
Deafly there
They heard nothing.
The current carried
Its cries downstream,
Rumours on the tide upward
Surged in triumph.
They did not notice.

We breathe them,
And telling their turbulent history
Realise that weirdly
They never knew their hinterland –
Only in us their marriage happens
And ours there somewhat –
In choruses of trees,
In the silence of full water,
They hold their dead, hold us,
Do not dissipate themselves,
Each locked intensely
In its own reach.

## THE ANATOMIST

Winter is lecturing.
He has taken over
The Chair of Necessary Studies.
And all things really
Constitute the lesson:
We have no choice
But to make ourselves available.

And, being human, we learn
Structures, relationships;
Could draw a tree almost,
Knowing piercingly how it stands
Like Burke's skeleton in the anatomy theatre.
The analogy is faulty:
Tree's flesh recovers.

Summer (easy in his five ounce suiting)
Is nowhere now. Through the fog, good smells
Of drink and dinner tempt our stomachs.
In the public-houses they have foreseen a coming
Even of idealists who smelling the hot meat hang their heads
Like those they ask a grace for – no toolmakers –
Laid quiet on our plates here.

STAR-GAZERS

Is it the absences (that dark is)
Make the light more tender,
The light dark crowds about?
To cut light into pools
With emptiness between
Urges a closeness here;
It comes with darkness crowding.
How know spark's tenement

But ride out darkness sometimes?
'Put off some of those lights':
Singleness blurs,
Boys' bonfire faces beam,
And – dared – nothingness rustles.
Or pooling all their years,
Time melted in this glow,
Aged kind eyes make remembered

Some occasion.
And half is darkness always:
When fireleap strikes the walls of some sad room
Or gleam of sun heals in a picture
Lost time to life again, or on a strand
Clouds race their charging shadows,
Then that thing unesteemed
Seems worthy,

As though dark's needed to see true,
Like far stars shining best
When earth's turned from her own,
As there at silent window,
Outriggered by the glow of homely candle
(for a sky's watch pinched out)
On nights clear of disturbance
Eyes took off lone across it. So must we.